WALKING BACKWARD

WALKING BACKWARD

Poems by

Diana Anhalt

Kelsay Books

Cover design: Shay Culligan

ISBN: 978-1-949229-94-3

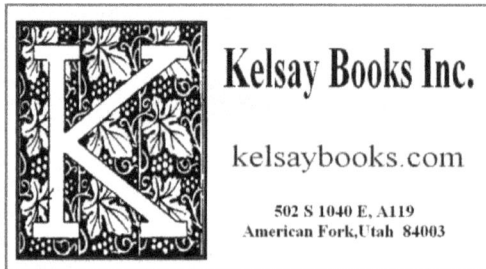

Kelsay Books Inc.

kelsaybooks.com

502 S 1040 E, A119
American Fork, Utah 84003

Para mi familia—for my family—Ricardo and Laura,
Judith and Paul,
and my granddaughters, Emma, Sarah and Bella

Acknowledgments

Anna Davidson Rosenberg Contest, Finalist, 2017
 "Family Tree, Annotated"
Avalon Literary Review
 "Measured Breathing"
 "On the Underground"
California Quarterly
 "About My Mother's Ears"
Common Ground Review
 "Manicure"
Connecticut River Review
 "Today"
Constellations
 "Afterthoughts"
 "The Family Name"
HazMat Review
 "To My Daughter Who Wants a Divorce"
Into the Teeth of the Wind
 "Blowing Lessons"
Kentucky Review
 "Inventory"
Lucid Stone
 "Instructions to My Husband on Choosing a Wife"
Main Street Rag
 "Duet"
Poem-Huntsville Literary Association/ First Prize,
*Georgia Poetry Society Contest, (*2018)
 "Homesick"
Poetica
 "My Uncle Abe Remembers his Crossing"
Poetry USA
 "Saplings"
Third Wednesday
 "Singing With My Father"

Contents

Walking Backward

Late each night, woozy with sleep, my bare feet
traveled blind—knew one room from the next

> through warps in the wood, space between
> floorboards. Sensed their width and breadth…

For forty years I called that place home.
It still resides in me. The feet are last to follow.

> They fumble with the unfamiliar, reject
> the waxed surface of a new life, are the last

to forgive my leaving, long to return me
to the old home—unwashed windows,

> lopsided gate, caged parrots in the kitchen,
> geraniums. At night my feet step back,

tread dream halls where faces linger in mirrors,
Spanish echoes down corridors into a past I left behind.

> And there you are, waiting in the entrance. You lean
> against the door frame, ask: *Como te fue? How did it go?*

Red wine or white?

Missing

I walk my unwritten poems down *La Reforma,*
stop to buy *La Prensa,* scan the Want Ads.
Missing bilingual parrot *Inglés/Español,*
answers to the name of *Palomitas.*

Se Busca María Felix look-alike for chachacha-ing
Saturday nights. *Extraviado/Lost* guitar case
filled with women's shoes and toothpaste samples.

In Search Of instructions on how to read divining bones.
Reward Offered for information leading to whereabouts
of Gabi Escobedo, missing since September.

Atención Mauricio—You've been dead long enough.
It's time to come home.

Afterthoughts

When you died Spanish followed you out
the door. So did our routine. I forgot to shop
on Wednesdays or make coffee your way.

I stopped winding your clock, no longer
laundered on Sundays. Today the scent
of sunlight's fled from our sheets

and I've grown deaf to the city's pulse,
wake to silence, draw the curtain shut
against morning. Sorrow hovers outside

our bedroom window, our bed widens.
It's your fault, of course. I intended
to die first, leave you free to marry

a girl young enough to outlive you.
And you? You just forged ahead,
refused to follow my plans.

Flashbacks

Suppose you find yourself in the middle of a flood.
Someone remarks, *But water is good for the plants,*

sounding exactly like your mother's cousin, Irma.
In that instant—some fifteen years dead—

she's back on board. Even those we barely knew
gate-crash, reappear in a gesture, their ability

to memorize telephone numbers, an allergy to cats.
They inhabit our rooms and their traits become ours

to discover in a stutter, a wink, a double-jointed finger,
the curvature of a spine. When my left hand thrums

the table like a keyboard we think of Uncle Abner. *He drove
us crazy.* Today, my dear, I look for you in our son—

in his gait, how he favors his right leg, folds the newspaper
in three. I study my daughter when she runs her hands

through her hair exactly as you did, throws back her head,
and cackles at her own jokes.

Family Tree, Annotated

It's all that remains of my family who lived
in the *shtetls* near Warsaw and Łódź—part of
Russia one day, Poland the next—who stayed
behind when the others left. Their letters ceased

after '42 so we burrow for memories gone to
seed, shake out branches for old-world names—
often misspelled—scribble lives onto paper
grown brittle with age. My grandfather's brother,

Maxim Zukowsky, worked as *a shochet,* in charge
of the ritual slaughter of chickens, married
to Channah. Her name's been crossed out. *No.*
He married Rebecca. *I think that she stuttered.*

There's a daughter, Rachel, *who eloped with*
a goy. Then a correction: *Nope. She married*
a boy who lived in Chelm. Eldest son, Herschel.
A Biblical scholar. As for the nephew—

Solly Zekowsky—*Involved in a plot to murder*
the Tsar. And Solly survived— No, you're wrong.
He was shot. Borris, *his brother, moved to New York,*
refused to learn English. Missed the sausage and borsht,

returned to his village in time for the war. And penned
in the margin: *They always told the same jokes twice,*
laughed 'til they cried. A note next to Shlomo, a cousin:
I think he turned off the light when they came for him.

Someone's added: *He probably took his violin.*

The Family Name

"Your name enters a room before you do.
Lingers after you're gone," my mother
used to say. "Remember. You're named
for your father, Moishe, Moishe Zhukovsky.
Gone now.

Allow this knowledge to sustain you—
Like a backbone, a conviction. Travel
his straight path. When you quit home
place your feet inside his shoes, make
his footsteps your own."

Today I thank God my mother never knew
that amid the jarring of foreign tongues,
children strayed. Bindles and baggage got
tossed aside, stomped underfoot, mislaid
in the shuffle.

An agent checked my papers, called me "Morris, Morris Zukof,"
wrote it down. Urged me on.

My Uncle Abe Remembers his Crossing—1912

We boarded the *Zeeland* in Antwerp, abandoned
our ragtag lives in exchange for a vision as slight
as a shadow, bearing what little was ours—
barley seeds from the garden in Vilna,
our family quilt, a bar of soap. I was five.

I carried the name I'd grown into pinned
to my shirt, one pair of shoes. We made
our way down into steerage while the band
played Viennese waltzes and dandies
on the upper deck waved hankies, blew kisses

to well-wishers on-shore. Berthed below with strangers
for more than sixteen days, we exchanged the reek
of vomit, coal dust lodged in our lungs, for salt-scented
breeze, sunshine's shimmer on water, and made
the lower deck our home.

My father pulled out his harmonica, played a polka or two
as first class passengers gazed down from above. I let
the music send its message to my feet, raised my arms
and danced. Saw my mother on her knees collecting
the shower of coins raining down on me.

Music Lessons

Little larger than a piano—
kitchen window view.

Aprons, work shirts hung
from makeshift clotheslines

strung along fire escapes. Late
afternoon, she'd stand there,

as sounds of tenement living—
slammed doors, trashcan lids,

chorus of Italian commands—
Subito. Vieni di sopra.

Yiddish curses—*far got's
tsulib haltn dos* resounded

through the courtyard. At times
ragged music—an easy-street

piano—drowned out the ruckus,
filled the flat with grandeur

and promise, compelled her
to seek out Macy's main floor

where a man in a Sunday tuxedo,
played Cole Porter favorites—

*Begin the Beguine, Easy to Love,
Let's Do It*—music to lift her

to the upper floors.

Translation

When I was a child, Spanish new to my tongue, *No pise el pasto—*
Don't step on the grass signs sprouted in Mexican parks.

My father translated: "Don't piss on the grass."
I believed him. Still didn't stop me from plopping, face down,

onto any green patch—sprigs prickling bare knees—
to press my nose into rain-dampened soil and swallow the taste

of dusty afternoons, breathe in the scent of the Bronx and strain
for the trolley's jangle, cry of the Good Humor man. We tied keys

around necks with red ribbon. They bounced against our chests.
Amid the frenzy of roller skates and bicycle bells, mothers

on benches, busy with babies or knitting—hurled the occasional
"Watch where you're going! Ya wanna get killed?"

Ear pressed to earth I listened, nibbled sweetness from a stem.
Grass whispered a language only my tongue understood.

My Father's Rules

New to Mexico, my father used to say,
Never shy from fear. Focus on traffic,
on strays, their bark. Take deep breaths.

     Back your bike away from open manholes,
     kids with sling shots. Keep your eyes peeled
     for the cliff's edge. Stare danger straight on.

A rooster crows as we leave our house
on *Callejón de las Cuatro Maravillas*.
A Mexican holiday. My parents sleep in.

     I help my sister with her skates, fasten mine
     and take off, my destination the farthest corner,
     leaving her behind to wobble between light poles.

When I turn I see a man. He approaches her, kneels,
reaches into his pocket—for candy, a gun?—I fasten
my gaze on him. Breathe in, breathe out, let fly.

     Slam into him, eyes screwed shut. Sink my teeth into
     his arm—taste sand, salt. Could it be blood? I spit. Later
     I'll ask my father, "What's the Spanish word for help?"

The Night My Mother Sang

A Quertéaro midnight—narrow highway—
car urged on by rumors of bandits and rockslides,
herds of groggy livestock on the road.

> "All we need now is rain," says my mother.
> Our headlights sweep past an endless procession
> of maguey. I'm scrunched in a corner at the back,

bare legs outstretched, clammy against plastic,
when our car skids, swerves from our lane.
My sister, head resting against the window, legs

> above mine, whimpers. My mother says,
> "Damn it Mike, watch where you're going."
> He steps on the gas. She starts to sing:

Oh what a beautiful morning, Oh what a beautiful day.
"To keep you awake," she says. Father punches the radio dial.
Para bailar la bamba, para bailar la bamba se necesita...

> She turns it off. "I told you to leave before 5:00."
> He pulls to the side of the road, "You drive then."
> She starts to cry. I decide not to tell them I have to pee.

Singing With My Father, 1952

At the corner of *Insurgentes* and *Michoacán* my father
double parks in front of *La Naval,* city's sole purveyor
of olive oil, saffron, sardines. He loosens his shoelaces,
blows his nose. "Stop kicking the seatback please."

The only sound a click-clack of signal lights. I roll down
the window to the scent of rain-washed pavement.
A new sky—tenuous clouds. "Three kids in my class
have ringworm." A burro stacked high with firewood

plods by. My father hums, *Plop, plop, fizz, fizz
oh what a relief it is...*I summon up long-ago car trips
when he drummed the dashboard to the beat of
Bongo, bongo, bongo, I don't wanna leave the Congo...

and start singing, softly at first, a hit parade tango stolen
from the Spanish: *Oh, when we're dancing and you're
dangerously near me, I get ideas, I get ideas...*My father
takes a comb to his mustache, catches my gaze

in the rearview mirror—*I want to hold you so much closer
than I dare to*—clears his throat, joins in: *I want to scold you
'cause I care more than I care to. And when I touch you
and there's fire in every finger...* My fingers scuttle across

the seatback, my feet thump against the floor—*I get ideas,
I get ideas.* I raise my voice, hurl our song out onto the street,
envision stiletto-heeled dancers in dresses slit to the hip,
tangoing alongside. An accordion player straddles the hood.

My father coughs. *I kind of think you get ideas…* Laden down with groceries, my mother peers in through the car window.

Note: The tango, *Adios, Muchachos,* was composed by Argentinean Julio Cesar Sanders in 1927. Dorcas Cochran published the English version in 1951.

Duet

A Sunday afternoon. I lie face down
in bed, my naked back your keyboard.
"Did I ever tell you I played the piano?"
you whisper. "With my twin brother.
We were ten. Wore short pants back
then. Our thighs stuck to the stool
while we bungled Liszt's Hungarian
Dance Number 2. How I hated it,
every do, re, mi, fa, sol of it,
the metronome's pulse in my ears,
while from the street, soccer playing
friends mocked us. My god. Awful!"

"What did you do?" "I sold the piano.
When my parents left town. Threw
in the portrait of Mendelssohn.
Kept the metronome. I think my
mother still has it." Today, when
I tell your story someone always
asks, "What did his parents say?"
I don't tell them that as your fingers
continued their glissando down
my spine, lingered in the curve
of my back, I never thought to ask.

Manicure

My mother-in law, who spoke with her hands, always avoided
shelling nuts, fondling pets. She prized her nails—impossibly long,
each groomed to a point, varnished with Sinfully Scarlet.
When I asked her why she took such pains, she spoke
of the well-born women of Linz:

"They removed kid gloves to reveal their hands—never sullied
by kitchen work. Bathed them daily in olive oil, wrapped them
nightly in flannel, while we—my sisters and me—skin roughened
by bleach and scouring soap, hid our nails behind our backs."

Today Huong Sang applies Baby's Blush: "Viet Nam lies under
yesterday's skies. But here I can order tomorrows.
Once the day comes when I'm rich like you, I'll grow my nails
two inches long, pay someone to give me a manicure."

Blowing Lessons

The wind hams it up tonight, barrels
its way through another performance,
rattles hangers in your empty closet,
tousles trees outside my window, hurtles

a nest into a shrub, feathers into haystacks.
I think of straw brooms, of gardeners
sweeping leaves away, the scattered leaves
of daily calendars, your first letters from camp.

The phone rings. I pick up the receiver, hear
your voice, whistling through the wires,
distorted by distance, as we rush to fill pauses
between sounds and comprehension.

Words swirl through the air. "We're getting
married in October," you say. I hesitate—
too long—then burst in, "My oh my!
How the years have flown-own-own…"

My voice echoes down the line. Wind flows
through the house, extinguishes the lights.
The line goes dead. As a baby such a wind
set you howling. You'd rise in your crib,

rattle the bars until I lifted you out. "Ssh,
it's only the wind-bird hooting the house
down. Whoo, whoo, whoo," I'd murmur,
and tighten my arms around you.

"Listen. It taps its beak against the window,
whirs wings against glass. Don't cry. Blow.
Blow like the wind bird. Whoo, whoo."
And as the wind rustled into nothingness,

I'd whisper, "See? Wind-bird has flown."
Tonight, your father fetches candles, strikes
matches on his shoe soles. They flare, unfurl
in the darkness like wings, return me

to the morning of your second birthday.
After breakfast, over spilt orange juice,
and bread crumbs I seat you on my knees
to rehearse your first public presentation.

Still in your pajamas, you blow banana milk
breath into my neck. I strike a match. You gasp.
"Now blow!" I cry, puffing my cheeks, releasing
a small gust into the palm of your hand.

"Happy birthday to you!" You reach for the match,
suck in your cheeks. I blow out a second, a third.
"Today we'll have ice cream, cake. Look! There's
a candle for Richard, a candle for mommy and one

for good luck." The pile of burnt matches grows.
"Blow, blow, blow like the wind bird. Whoo, whoo."
The wind's whispering now, spurting in gusts, wafting
back on itself, coming to rest. Wind-bird has flown.

Saplings

Saplings don't belong in car trunks.
This one protested, leaves quivering,

spine arching bow-like, resenting perhaps,
entombment with the unstrung guitar,

shiny garden tools, road maps stiff in wrappers.
So I stowed it in the back seat with the children.

They squatted beneath tear-shaped leaves
engineering tree-houses, planting forests,

aping gorillas. Trees along *Reforma* float, fuzzed
by gas fumes, pencil scrawls hastily erased.

The city crouches on my fender, claws
at the windshield. I roll up the windows.

Babes in the wood, forests sprout in your heads.
Your twitter helps mute the siren's shriek.

As your days lift leafy with promise, I promise
not to tell you what I know.

What I don't know about soccer

would fill a stadium. At least, that's what my nephew thinks:
"*Tia,* you don't even know what a penalty is." Stolid on little boy
legs, arms out-spread, he guards the goal post—a hassock
and kitchen stool set three feet apart—his uniform Mexico's colors,
green, red, white.

Clothed in baggy kneed tights, tie-dyed tee-shirt, pink curlers,
and wariness, I defend the other end, flanked by two chairs.
He dodges across the room, urges the ball forward. I block,
dislodge it from his instep, sideswipe and send it weaving
drunkenly between the chairs.

"GOOOOOOL! Hey. I scored!" "No. It's mine. That's my goal.
One-zero." I toss him the ball from the side-line. He blocks it with
his knee, teases it across the linoleum, easing it into the end zone.
It skids by me. "GOOOOOOL!" He raises his hands above his
head, spreads his fingers into vees. "Two-zero. Yay! Hooray!

Gosh, you're terrible, *tia.*" He's right. My incompetence boggles.
What I don't know about soccer would fuel legends. What I do
know are mornings tasting of wind, sand and crushed spring grass,
slippery underfoot, the itch of sun-dried mud on bare flesh,
sweat-stung eyes, the vain jabs at an elusive ball caught

in a thicket of legs, the throb of a bruised shin, of defeat.
I also know that moment when the field spreads out before you,
lonely as a blank page, and the ball squirms free. You're dribbling.
Ball bonds with foot. Heart-thump matches footfall. You're tugged
goal-ward as if by a force outside your self. You pass, receive,

and pass again in a pattern as fluid as speech with a symmetry
all its own. No. I won't tell him. Some things can not be taught.
I only hope he grows to meet that instant, startling as a slap

when your body rises skyward, the ball jolts against your forehead, with the urgency of inspiration: Athena springing full-blown from Zeus's head, a moment when header becomes poem.

Instructions to my Husband on Choosing a Wife

Dear,

When I leave, look for a woman resembling
the one who camps in my body sporadically
or journeys through it, a nomad, startling us
with a nudge or guffaw not my own.

One of ten children, she can catch a fast ball
without flinching, bake bread, knit, cry,
but never for herself. Doesn't write. Flares
her nostrils when annoyed, believes in God.

Were I not on guard I might become her,
and, at times, sense her presence settling
in the folds beneath my breasts, creases
between my thighs. She carries the scent

of rain and freshly washed sheets, never turns
from blood. She reminds me of the woman
who lived in your mother's eyes, had no
reason to lie, never solicited flattery.

When I leave, find this woman—Marry her.

On the Underground

They shuffle onto our train at Saint-Denis.
The crowd jostles her tambourine and when
he lifts the bow to his violin she starts to sing—
La Vie en Rose. Stumbles over words. Her voice
cracks. She starts again.

They're our age at least. He wears a tie. Shirt collar's
frayed. Her sweater's patched, scarf wrinkled—
possibly *Hermés.* Do you remember? Our last trip
to Paris? A bad time—stock market plunging,
you newly retired. We went anyway.

I fix my eyes on the couple and fumble for change.
Passengers look away. You read my mind
and say, *My God! Imagine. Having to scrape by
on a stranger's pennies. And I don't even play the violin.*

About My Mother's Ears

I shouted to be heard.
Why do you whisper?
Speak up, speak up,
my mother cried.

Don't you know nothing is lonelier than silence?
But our exchanges blurred, tenuous as organza,
yesterday's promises, smoke. After her operation
she expected sounds she hadn't heard in twenty years:

clatter of typewriter keys, kind words, heavy breathing—
to enter her ears politely—like reception-line guests
or nuns on their way to mass. Instead, she got barbarians,
buzz saws, operatic thunder, firing squads, family feuds.

Stop shouting at me! Stop pounding on my door! Today,
as occasional stray truths slither through or gnat-like circle
her head, she cries *Give me back my silence please,*
I need to think.

My Father-in-Law at the Beach

You kneel to fasten your father's sandals. He hovers above you,
gazes benignly as you fumble with his pea-green socks.

"I thought engineers were good with their hands," he chirps,
and drops like some exhausted puppet back into his beach chair.

You smile at me and shrug. I gesture to your right. A teenager
buried in sand lifts her head to giggle as her boyfriend kneads

two enormous boobs above her own. He scoops up sand in fistfuls,
strokes it into place, studs both nipples with bottle caps.

"I'm going back to Munich," he says. "My son promised."
You reach out to pat his arm. "Could be there were survivors."

Behind us, bougainvillea bleeds onto white walls. "The Nazis
would have killed her anyway, even if I'd sent the money.

Don't look at me that way!" He clutches the arm of his chair
with one hand, plucks the air with the other, observes the play

of his fingers. "Look! They've stolen my watch again.
Those bastards!"

To My Daughter Who Wants a Divorce

You call me long distance, and tell me in your five-year-old voice:
"My one-year-old marriage sucks." What you're really saying is,

you don't want to wake up twenty years from now, in the same bed
with this good, dull man and discover you didn't run for president,

save the Amazon. Shit! You didn't even balance your checkbook,
give to Amnesty International, return your library books on time.

I hear your sobbing, the silences in between. You pause for breath.
The mouth of my womb contracts. What should I say? "Good God!

We gave you everything. Ballet lessons, straight teeth, an M.A.
What did we do wrong?" Perhaps, I should remind you

of my single friends, masturbating in their bathtubs, answering
'personals' in the *Village Voice,* playing footsy with your father

under the table. Should I be flip? "Great idea darling. You've heard
of double weddings? How about a double divorce?" Or echo

my mother: "Darling, marriage, children. What more could you
want? It's only a matter of time. Just look at your father and me..."

Bella

You died young, were known for your irreverence.
Years later my daughter names her daughter for you.
I wonder why. Does she remember your small frame
scurrying through life clutching a handbag?

When I hear your name will I recall the coffee
on your breath, your selective hearing, fingers
toying with pianos or tightening around my arm?
Perhaps she'll inherit your left-handed gene,

your disheveled eyebrows, gap-toothed smile,
and, like you, live for lost causes, screw her eyes
shut at the sight of blood, or lie awake, listening
to the watchman blowing his night whistle.

Like most of us, you may be easy to forget.
You forgot nothing: your Venus flytrap memory
snapped shut around a random address or affront.
I'll search for you in her, hope she lives longer,

laughs louder, learns to dance.

About Teaching a Granddaughter How
to Cartwheel

She's six. I'm sixty-two, flunked gymnastics at MSU
but consider myself an expert at everything else—
like telling people what to do and how to do it.

We Google: *The cartwheel is a split hand movement.*
"Do you know what that means?" she asks. "Of course,"
I say. And instruct her to raise her arms above her head,

place one foot behind the other. "Think hand, hand,
foot, foot. Let the front leg take the weight, bend
to your right." My hands meet around her waist. I flip

her over. We start again. I do what I do best. I talk.
Of dancers and muscle memory, movements stored
in limbs…She rolls her eyes. "Look," I say:

"Once your feet discover their plan…" Does she listen?
It's like writing poetry, a matter of faith. Words do
their own thing, take center stage, turning cartwheels

of their own across the blank field of the page.

Inventory

Between the two of us we manage to hold on to almost all
we need to know. You keep track of 27 bridge conventions,
the formula for converting centigrade to Fahrenheit, shortcuts,
losses, how to light my pilot, change a tire.

I get to remember our first date, the kids' close calls, lyrics
to *Oklahoma,* my mother's grip on my elbow, the words in French
for 'Where is the bathroom?,' how not to change a tire. Along
with recollections of sand, hot beneath bare feet, odor of ozone

after lightening storms, a stranger's compliment, a squabble
in a parking lot, our battalion of etceteras thrives, takes up
residency in the back yard. It lays down roots. Like bamboo
that burrows beneath the house, loosens tiles on the kitchen floor,

reappears in the bedroom, it survives, barring dementia or demise.
I'd like to believe that once we're gone we'll leave behind some
memories of ourselves lined up in rows like visitors' shoes outside
a temple door.

Measured Breathing

In bed in this dark room you're invisible and silent,
like bones beneath flesh. Weighted down by sleep,

I place my head on your shoulder, willing the tempo
of my breathing to echo the meter of your own.

I scan its prosody, memorize you. A faucet drips.
Seconds spill from the clock—one, two, three, four…

numbered like our days. How many heartbeats
to a minute? Sixty-five? Eighty? How many to a day?

A bell tolls nine times in the graveyard. I count,
fingers clamped tight around this moment.

A blur of headlights glances off the wall. As I listen
to the urgency of early morning traffic, I know

that someday, should I remain alone, I'll choose
to sleep on your side of the bed, tally up my gains.

Today,

if you entered the study in search
of your glasses or to call my attention to a hawk
perched on the terrace railing or a full moon,
your slippers flapping against the wooden floor,

I'd tell you I ransacked our apartment for directions—
How to navigate from 'Married' to 'Widow'
on government forms, revisit our past without a map.
I never learned the coordinates of solitude,

where to find myself when your absence
sheds its silence down our hall. But sometimes
I step from the shower, catch your eye
in the steamy bathroom mirror.

Wait for you to hand me
a towel.

Empty Chair

This morning at breakfast, my muse plopped down,
took over the chair my love left empty
and I wanted to say, "Hey, that seat's taken."
She reached for my coffee, started to nag.

I gave you sounds to swim in, fielded your silences,
steadied your wobbling will... "Oh please," I replied,
and got up to wash the dishes. *You loved me once.*
My words wandered through your head like sheep.
We herded them together...

"Spare me the clichés," I said. "You can do better."
She persisted: *He won't return but if you open*
the windows when it rains... I struggled to explain—
"When my love died, life moved to a street
my feet can't find."

Homesick

We never thought we'd miss
the church bells grown delirious
by Sunday or the cries of *basura,*
basura hurled into the street
from Mexico City's garbage trucks
or our first home where scorpions
rallied in the bathtub and the bamboo
thrust through parquet floors.
We'd remember how afternoon air
held an odor all its own—pungent
with roasted chilies, dust and diesel oil—
how our ears were still attuned
for the knife sharpener's whistle,
for the vendors touting their wares—
pineapples, ice, live turkeys—how
our tongues knew to fondle
the r's in *ferrocarril* and yes—even
the urgency of early morning news
blasted onto the street from
loud-speaker trucks. We longed
for that too. But today I miss most
the everyday words time's stripped
from my tongue, the *tu* and the *yo,*
the you and the me.

When Our Shoes Take Us

Jews should be born with the wind at their backs and wheels
on their heels like taxicabs.

—My grandmother

If we fled Sevilla, Podolia, Uzbekistan, Kiev on a day of sun,
we'd sling our shoes around our necks by their laces, relish
the prickle of grass against naked soles, let our feet scrawl
messages in the dust of our pasts, of lives left behind.

We saved what shoes we had for snow, gravel, seemliness.
Our featherbeds, a Kiddush cup, a violin, perhaps, we strapped
to our backs, and the stories of ancestors—their feet caked
in the clay of Judea, Canaan, Goshen, Galilee—rode

our tongues. Our fate? To change nations more often
than shoes, store yesterday's crumbs in our pockets. To leave
our children small things that fit into suitcases: a menorah,
a teapot, a cameo brooch, photo of somebody's grave.

Look, a clutch of letters, scent of memories. No pianos,
no grandfather clocks, no grandfathers. One pair of shoes.

About the Author

Diana Anhalt left Mexico over nine years ago following close to a lifetime in that country but claims her writing sometimes digs in its heels and refuses to budge. She continues to write about Mexico. Many of her essays, short stories, and book reviews have appeared in both English and Spanish along with her book, *A Gathering of Fugitives: American Political Expatriates in Mexico 1948-1965.*

Since she first arrived in Atlanta, two of her chapbooks, *Second Skin,* (Future Cycle Press), *Lives of Straw,* (Finishing Line Press), and one short collection, *Because There Is No Return,* (Passager Books), have been published. Her work has been nominated for a Pushcart Prize and has appeared in "Nimrod," "Concho River Review," "The Connecticut River Review," "The Atlanta Review," and "Spillway," among many others. She believes this is the first time her work has started to lose its Mexican accent.

I particularly want to thank Karen Kelsay and Shay Culligan
of Kelsay Books for their patience, hard work
and invaluable support and my daughter-in-law, Carrie Crane,
for her painstaking assistance and encouragement.

www.ingramcontent.com/pod-product-compliance
Lightning Source LLC
LaVergne TN
LVHW091321080426
835510LV00007B/597